Lion on the Inside

How One Girl Changed Basketball

WRITTEN BY
Bilqis Abdul-Qaadir with Judith Henderson

ILLUSTRATED BY
Katherine Ahmed

A collection of books that inform children about the world and inspire them to be engaged global citizens

Kids Can Press

There's a hoop up there,
   in the air.
Waiting. Daring you.
Come on! Take the shot!

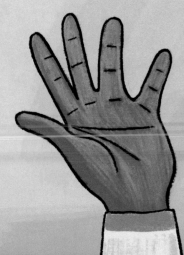

Flick-a-the-wrist.
Ball on a mission.
No sound sweeter.
SWISH!
Clean through the rim.
IN.

My name is Bilqis Abdul-Qaadir.
Qisi for short.
I was born into a basketball team.
A family of love and faith.
I was born strong, like my mom.
Strong like Mudgie — my grandmother
    and loudest cheerleader.

When I'm three, I'm a pro!

I have my own hoop in the house.

But my brothers keep butting in.

They block and elbow.

"MINE!" I bellow.

"Foul!" cries our referee. "Free throw for Qisi!"

"DO WHAT YOU DO! DUNK IT!"
Mudgie cheers.
SWISH!

When I'm seven,
   I win the Dining Room Game of Fame.
We're all munching on Mudgie's chewy
   chocolate chip cookies.
"I can hit the basket from here," I declare.
"Yeah, right," says Sef.
"Bet my cookie you can't," says Suli.

But I'm a pro.
One-handed throw.
Ball on a mission.
Over the cookies, the candlesticks,
  the tulips, the cat
  and Ping, the fish.
SWISH!
"Give it up, Suli."

At twelve, I try on my mom's favorite hijab.
"How do I look?"
"Beautiful."

I slap my favorite cap on top. "How about this?"
"Pretty cool."
"I'm gonna go play hoops."

There's Mr. Bigshot, all strut and swagger.
Hogging the hoop, as usual.
I dribble and drive.
Deke and whirl.
Jump. Take the shot.
SWISH!
"Not bad for a girl." Mr. Bigshot smirks.

I'm steamed.

"Really?" I throw again.

Clean through the rim. IN.

Mr. Bigshot snickers.

"What's with the ugly scarf?"

"This scarf? It's my superpower."

I shoot again.
Mr. Bigshot snatches the ball from the air.
"Come and get it."
He dribbles. He charges.
I go down. Get back up. "Foul!"

I nab the ball.
Pivot past him. Drive to the basket. Lay up the shot,
     give him the eyeball
     and leave.

Mom is calm.

Me, not so much.

"He charged at me! I should've pushed back."

"I'm glad you walked away."

"And I played better!"

"That's no surprise."

"And he called your headscarf ugly."

"Let THEM talk. YOU play ball."

Mom is quiet confidence.

"Pick your battles, Bilqis."

At fourteen, I'm in high school.
I'm a Wildcat.
And I have my own hijab.

GO WILDCATS GO!

Wild hair under there!
My lion on the inside.
My hijab reminds me every day —
    do the right thing.
I am fierce.
I am faithful.
I am kind.

At seventeen,

I'm the star player on our varsity team.

It's the day of the playoffs.

My family is in the stands.

I can hear Mudgie. Who can't?!

"DO WHAT YOU DO!"

It's tip-off time.

But then ...

"Number 1! You can't play with the scarf."

"What do you mean? Why?"

"It's the rules."

"This is a hijab. I can't take it off."

"Then you can't play."

The Wildcats go wild.
"WHAT!"
"WHY?"
"NO WAY!"
The referee is blowing.
I'm steaming.

I desperately want to play.
Maybe I could take it off ...
   just this once.
I mean, it doesn't change
   who I am.
I look over at my mom, so calm.
Mudgie, not so much.
"THAT'S FOUL! FOUL!"
I'm thinking, *Pick your battles.*

And I know in my heart ...
I'm not going to play.

Then the Wildcats grab me by the elbows.
Arm in arm,
    we all stand firm at center court.
The crowd is loud.
The referees huddle.

The whistle blows.
"Okay! Play ball!"
And I do.

SWISH!

My 3070th point!
I become the all-time lead scorer —
    girl or boy —
    in Massachusetts State history.

I get a full scholarship to the
    University of Memphis.
Play my final season at Indiana State.
I'm the first woman to wear a hijab
    in NCAA history.

The leader of the free world notices.
He invites me to play hoops at his house.
Not boasting or anything, but I win.
The president is a really good sport.

MUSLIM GIRLS HOOP TOO

I'm ready.
Ready to move on.
Ready to take on the world!
Ready to play international pro basketball.
But then
   it happens again.

"Number 10. You can't play."

"WHAT! NO WAY! WHY?"

"The rules. You can't play with a headscarf."

My heart stops.

Why does this keep happening?

Why are they forcing me to choose?

WHY WON'T THEY LET ME DO WHAT I DO?

Why?

The bouncing of the ball
   is the beating of my heart.
But my faith is my heart, too.
I could remove my hijab ...
   I could take it off and play.
I could.

But that wouldn't be me.
So I choose.
I choose not to play.
That day changes my life forever.
And my heart
   is
   broken.

I picked my battle.
After three years,
    after thousands of letters ...
    we win.
The rule that bans headscarves
    is overturned.
But it's too late for me.
Too late to play pro basketball
    on the world stage.

Today,
I have more dreams,
    and I have the power.
To teach.
To inspire.
To lead.
My wish, my mission —
    every Muslim girl,
    every girl,
    knows she has a shot.
Take it!

Flick-a-the-wrist.
No sound sweeter.
SWISH!
Clean through the rim.
IN.

Meet Bilqis Abdul-Qaadir

> **"Bilqis is an inspiration not simply to Muslim girls — she's an inspiration to all of us."**
>
> — *President Barack Obama*

> **"Sometimes the paths on our journey are difficult, but remember that we are making the paths easier for those who will follow."**
>
> — *Bilqis Abdul-Qaadir*

Bilqis Abdul-Qaadir was born and raised in a Muslim family in Springfield, Massachusetts, the birthplace of basketball. She is the youngest of eight children in her family. Bilqis started playing basketball when she was only three years old, and she's been playing ever since.

Bilqis began wearing her hijab every day when she was in high school. She currently holds the Massachusetts State high school basketball scoring record, with 3070 points! Bilqis later became the first Muslim woman to play NCAA (National Collegiate Athletic Association) Division I basketball wearing a hijab. She was invited to the White House three times and was recognized by President Barack Obama for her achievements.

Bilqis trained hard and made it to the professional basketball level. However, the professional league had a rule prohibiting headgear larger than five inches, which meant she would not be allowed to wear her hijab on the court. So, Bilqis had to choose between her faith and the sport she loved.

She chose her faith, advocated for Muslim women and girls in sports through her nonprofit organization Muslim Girls Ball Too (formerly Muslim Girls Hoop Too), and played a key role in pushing the professional league, FIBA (International Basketball Federation), to change their rule regarding headgear. That happened in 2017. Today, Bilqis is an athletic director, motivational speaker and sports trainer, creating sports programs, leagues and opportunities for Muslim girls and boys internationally.

Bilqis playing her final collegiate season at Indiana State University.

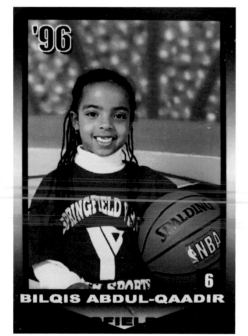

BILQIS ABDUL-QAADIR

Bilqis's YMCA player photo from 1996.

Let's Talk

1. For Bilqis, her Muslim faith and basketball are very important. What things are most important to you? Why?

2. Bilqis says she is strong like her mother and her grandmother. Do you share similarities with someone in your family? What qualities do you have in common?

3. Bilqis's Wildcats teammates refuse to play without Bilqis. If you saw something you thought was unfair happening to someone else, what are some ways you could help?

4. Bilqis's mother tells her to pick her battles. What do you think this means? Have you ever had to make this kind of choice?

5. What do you think it means to have a "lion on the inside"?

Discover More

Behind This Basketball Scoring Leader's Fight to Play. Great Big Story. Available at youtu.be/xlewyGcP1qc.

"Bilqis Abdul-Qaadir, Basketball Player & Speaker." BAM/Book a Muslim. Available at bookamuslim.com/bilqis-abdul-qaadir.

"Bilqis Abdul Qaadir." Mark Chiarelli. Available at theblackamericanmuslim.com/bilqis.

Life Without Basketball Official Trailer. Pixela Pictura Films. August 2, 2016. Available at youtu.be/OavrXZs9YgM.

"2021 NCAA Final Four Talks Full Panel." NCAA.com. Available at youtu.be/nM2gIA9DDkl.

"This Muslim Basketball Player Refused to Take off Her Hijab, Opening New Doors for Athletes of Other Faiths." Alaa Elassar. CNN, November 7, 2020.

Citizen Kid ™

Dear Reader,

We hope that this book has sparked thoughtful questions and inspirational conversations about what it means to make a difference.

Developed by Kids Can Press, the CitizenKid collection encourages young readers to learn about global issues and then think about ways that they can help improve the communities they live in, and the world at large.

CitizenKid is 25 books strong, with more to come. Almost 2 million copies have been sold to date, and the collection has been translated into 27 languages. CitizenKid books have garnered worldwide critical acclaim.

Each CitizenKid book is developed with one or more of the United Nations Sustainable Development Goals (SDG) in mind, such as climate action, clean water and sanitation, gender equality, poverty and more. The Goals are a universal call to action to end poverty, protect the planet and improve the lives and prospects of everyone, everywhere.

For our part, Kids Can Press is a proud signatory of the UN's SDG Publisher's Compact. The Compact is designed to accelerate progress to achieve the Goals through publishing books that support positive change.

How will you help change the world?

#CitizenKid

To my grandmother, Mudge, The Matriarch, our butterfly, you are sorely missed.
Thank you for instilling love, strength and most importantly faith, in my life. *I love you more.*

To my first-born niece, Amany, my mini me, my protégé. I pass the ball to you. Dribble it toward greatness,
whether that's on or off the court. Your purpose is BIG, and I pray this book inspires you to fulfill it.

To my Queen, my mother, my "Umi," thank you isn't enough. I could write an entire book about you,
your courage, your leadership and your strength. I still — and will always — want to be like you,
and I pray I've made you proud.

— B.A-Q.

To Debbie Rogosin. SWISH! — J.H.

For Sahar and Loujane — K.A.

CitizenKid™ is a trademark of Kids Can Press Ltd.

Published in Canada and the U.S. by Kids Can Press Ltd.
25 Dockside Drive, Toronto, ON M5A 0B5

Kids Can Press is a Corus Entertainment Inc. company

www.kidscanpress.com

The artwork in this book was rendered digitally in Procreate.
The text is set in Albert Sans.

Edited by Debbie Rogosin
Designed by Marie Bartholomew

Printed and bound in Buji, Shenzhen,
China, in 3/2023 by WKT Company

CM 23 0 9 8 7 6 5 4 3 2 1

Photo credit: Page 38 (top) photographed by Drew Canavan;
used with permission of Indiana State University.

FSC
www.fsc.org
MIX
Paper | Supporting
responsible forestry
FSC® C010256

Library and Archives Canada Cataloguing in Publication

Title: Lion on the inside : how one girl changed basketball /
Bilqis Abdul-Qaadir with Judith Henderson ; illustrated by
Katherine Ahmed.
Names: Abdul-Qaadir, Bilqis, author. | Henderson, Judith, author. |
Ahmed, Katherine, illustrator.
Description: Includes bibliographical references.
Identifiers: Canadiana (print) 20220468648 | Canadiana
(ebook) 20220468702 | ISBN 9781525310034 (hardcover) |
ISBN 9781525311611 (EPUB)
Subjects: LCSH: Abdul-Qaadir, Bilqis — Juvenile literature. |
LCSH: Women basketball players — United States — Biography —
Juvenile literature. | LCSH: Basketball players — United States —
Biography —Juvenile literature. | LCSH: Muslim athletes —
United States — Biography — Juvenile literature. | LCSH: Hijab
(Islamic clothing) — Juvenile literature. | LCGFT: Autobiographies.
Classification: LCC GV884.A23 A3 2023 | DDC j796.323092—dc23

Kids Can Press gratefully acknowledges that the land on which
our office is located is the traditional territory of many nations,
including the Mississaugas of the Credit, the Anishnabeg, the
Chippewa, the Haudenosaunee and the Wendat peoples and is
now home to many diverse First Nations, Inuit and Métis peoples.

We thank the Government of Ontario, through Ontario Creates,
the Ontario Arts Council; the Canada Council for the Arts; and
the Government of Canada for supporting our publishing activity.